UNDER THE SUN OUR HEARTS ARE BEATING

BY

SEKI LYNCH

Salamander Street

First published in 2024 by Salamander Street Ltd.
(info@salamanderstreet.com)

A CIP catalogue record for this book is available from the British Library.

Cover and interior illlustration by: Tom Maryniak

ISBN: 9781739103040

10 9 8 7 6 5 4 3 2 1

Wordville

If it plucks a chord when you read this,
this book is for you.
Whether you understand why or not,
this book is for you.
Find me at the feast, where it won't matter what we
remember or forget.
With every fibre of love,
Thank you

ABOUT SEKI LYNCH

Don't worry, my name's dead easy. It's like, "say hi" with a 'k'. I usually do that with a wave. Hiya!

I'm a performance poet, author, lyricist and playwright from Leeds. My first book, *Ten Drinks That Changed the World*, was published globally by ACC Art Books in 2018. It's a book about the history of spirits (booze, not ghosts).

Barber B: A Play of Sorts, was my debut stage production, co-created with a barber—Leeds legend, Brian Swarray... but that's a story for another time.

This is my first collection of poems. I perform them onstage unaccompanied and with jazz musicians. Venues of note I've performed at include the V&A Museum, the Leeds Playhouse and the Henry Moore Institute (whilst barefoot). At some point, I'll finish one of the novels I've started. Until then, I'm sharing these poems in the hope they might help you feel a little less alone.

Take care fellow human consciousness.

FOREWORD

Being a prose man, I may be underqualified to introduce these poems. Still, I was glad to be asked, because the experience of reading them has raised the spirits, and caused wonder.

These are poems to live with, learn from. Most of them are new to me; but even from recent acquaintance, I think I've noticed an essential theme, and a manner of thinking and feeling in them. They are often concerned with nature, earthly and cosmic; but as they stretch the imagination to cycles and vast forces, they are also moving homewards to a present in which the poet has a partner in the poem; which partner could also be you or I, the reader. This is a loving movement. Take these lines:

> We were two snowflakes in the blizzard
> Until we melted back into the sea
>
> Do you remember anything
> Before we got home? ['Home']

Note the passage from the sublime in the first two lines (with their Faustian note) to the practical world of late-night drinking in the next two. And the familiar register recurs, amid the starry speculations:

> As the world turns underfoot—nothing's far
> The brilliance of your happiness in bloom
> Fill's my mind's sky with galaxies
> Snowflakes on tar. ['Strings']

In this movement between the vast, the everyday and the personal consists, I'm noticing, the remarkable self-consciousness of the poems; also, their wisdom. It is a wisdom of heart and mind. For me, these elements illustrate some words of Maurice Merleau-Ponty: 'The world is wholly inside and I am wholly outside myself.'

In reading the collection, I thought to myself, 'Now this is the key poem!' Thought it again—and again. Which testifies to the strength of the poems gathered here. 'The Feast' was one which affected me in this way; its combination of dream, banquet, drink, fire and ecstatic merging confirmed for me that these poems had passed Nietzsche's cardinal test for art: 'Regarding all aesthetic values I now avail myself of this main distinction: I ask in every instance, "is it hunger or superabundance [*Der Überfluß*] that has here become creative?"' It is superabundance, overflow, that has motivated these poems—their dancing, flexible, cheerful gratitude. In this sense, they are making contact with that most challenging of art and life criteria that Nietzsche termed the 'Dionysian.' And I think this holds even of the most awe-inspiring poem here, "Oumuamua', in which an eel-shaped rocky body from beyond the Solar System eavesdrops on us all.

'O God, I could be bounded in a nutshell and count myself a king of infinite space—were it not that I have bad dreams.' That was a complaint of Prince Hamlet's. Are there bad dreams, regrets, among these poems? Perhaps. But unlike Hamlet, Seki Lynch seems to have overcome them. Reading the poems should make you want to know the man who wrote them; I'm happy to say I do (I think!)

Michael Nath
2024

INTRODUCTION

Well, you made it!

I don't know what's called you to open up this little book of my musings, but welcome! Beyond this introduction is a poetic exploration of my hopes, fears, loves and losses written across about a decade. Since you made it this far—considering buying a poetry collection for yourself or someone else—I suspect this life has been something of a ride for you too. Don't worry if you want to skip ahead, but for those interested enough, let me explain why I'd like to share this gathering of my consciousness with you...

I fell in love with poetry at 17, reading T.S. Eliot's 'The Love Song of J. Alfred Prufrock'. Before then, interactions in my life often left me wanting. I felt as if we were all living a kind of pantomime. There was a sense our true thoughts and feelings were buried under our makeup and costumes. I had this deep yearning to connect that I couldn't express, let alone fulfil. Eliot's words, in their fragmented, nonsensical gibberish, spoke to me in a way that lit me up. They resonated with familiarity and fed in me the thing which was famished. Eliot's work helped me feel understood when I felt deeply lonely. How could a dead person with such a different lived experience from mine make me feel so seen, so validated, so connected? I wanted to learn how he'd done that—made me feel a little less alone. Perhaps one day, I thought, I might do the same.

As I discovered more poets, authors, music and ideas, I found that these too helped me relate to myself and the world around me. Magpie that I am, I collected these gleaming shards within. When I felt lost or sought comfort,

I returned to these inner adornments. Sure of their power, with lesser or greater camouflage, I used them to bolster my own strange mosaics. In part, because I felt unable to match their beauty. In part, as a means of passing them on to others. Having gathered, processed and reconstituted for some time now, I thought I might share a collection of my own, with the hope of inspiring connection.

Sitting down to write this introduction, I haven't been able to avoid a pervasive feeling in my life. I wonder if you feel it too, this terrific loneliness? Beyond all evidence of family, friends and deep loves, it remains. But it's far from the only thing I feel. I feel unfathomable hope for myself and humanity. Right now, genocides are happening. People are passing in and out of this world. There are people discovering heartbreak and people finding out they don't have long to live. On micro and macro scales, we live with griefs, sorrows and disappointments that might cause us to despair. Any given day might see us fade out whilst sipping on the low wines of bitterness and regret. I'm guilty of this sipping. My loneliness has been a habitual intoxicant. However, I also feel immeasurable joy. I feel oneness and grandness and possibility. Now and then, I swoon at the realisation that all this is happening. That I'm on this journey with others. That, wherever life force comes from, if only a natural occurrence in the universe, to be conscious of our own existence is still a phenomenal gift.

The beautiful cover of this book, designed by my dear friend Tom Maryniak, captures this multiplicity perfectly. At first, I wasn't sure about how the trees imposed themselves on those feasting in the woods. I'd wanted the cover to be wholly joyous, wholly celebratory... I sat with the image. I showed a lover. I reflected. A joyous image wouldn't have told the whole truth of what these poems mean to me, or of what I hope they might mean to you. There are many moments of joy and hope in this collection but it also inhabits darkness. I hope the poems can bring some comfort, some light, some rest and relief to those who might be struggling in the dark.

I was born four months premature. My parents thought I was a miracle (I know...). Even if you were born on your due date, without incident, people far cleverer than I have worked out that the chances of you being here are 1 in $10^{2,685,000}$. Now, I'm no mathematician, but I reckon if you filled this book with 0s, you'd run out of room trying to get to that number. In simple terms, you had no chance. But, here you are, reading my book.

Giving these poems is a way of trying to connect with that. To say, despite the sometimes insufferable weight of existence, you still have breath entering your lungs and blood pumping through your heart and this is enough. There is wind in the trees and the water which fills our oceans has passed through every living creature that's ever existed, including you. There may be days when you feel so far from life and people that it may not seem worth it. You may not feel worthy enough to be part of the great dance. But as deep as despair may take you or as far away as you may feel, you are a part of this maelstrom of life and you will be after you've taken your last breath. You'll disintegrate back into the oceans and your particles will carry on the breezes to be inhaled by billions more people and creatures. You are a part of the great wheel that turns. There is life current within you and it hopes you might go on.

This collection is a call to celebrate in the face of all our anxieties, barriers, hang-ups, misunderstandings and fears. It's a call to celebrate that for a short time, on this tiny speck of rock with a molten heart, we shared our consciousness and current with a few hundred billion organisms. Against all odds, we were here under the sun and our hearts were beating.

Seki Lynch
2024

CONTENTS

A gathering of consciousness from
Seki Lynch

HOMECOMING

Welcome back say the roots of the tree to the rains

How we've missed you...

Take shelter within us for a little while

Let's trade stories—before the doors of our pores open
once more. And you return to the rain-rich skies

Welcome says the cliff face through a billion years of tears

Welcome says the bloods plasma as it constantly refreshes

Welcome says the enzyme-rich saliva, dust-speckled and
fungi-spored

Welcome say the planets as they return once more from
the outer limits of their orbits

Always coming back

Always coming back around

Each of us an intertwining orchestra of birth and death
whose music affects the symphonies of others. Gather
'round this fire and let your music pour

Yes, come gather 'round

The journey is never-ending but gather here a moment with me

We're on our way, returning to the tides

We're on our way from the moment we're alive

On our way, returning to the tides

On our way from the moment we're alive

When was the last time you lit a fire, my love?

Do you remember?

ALL COMES BACK AROUND

*Dedicated to Brian Swarray, master barber and Leeds legend. The poem closed our stage production **Barber B: A Play of Sorts**.*

It all comes back around
Textures and sounds
Things thought lost, now found
It all comes back around

Movement of the galaxy's swirl
Twisting 'round as hair curls
Monkey puzzle to pine cone pearls
Planets spinning as life whirls
It all comes back around

Wisdom in the hermit's shell
Frequency of wedding bells
Rhythm and pitch are one as well
Only truth is time will tell
It all comes back around

Humans, natural pattern makers
Making patterns ever greater
Life has its givers and its takers
Friends once close become distant later
It all comes back around

The current and the giggling stream
The ever-expanding universe seams
The ones we miss we find in dreams
And some arrive as others leave
It all comes back around

Begin a job for a new car
Nick others, rubber screech on tar
It could have been so different star
Did you ever imagine how far?
It all comes back around

Golden ratio of half and half
Unique cowhide of cow and calf
The human race; a mixture of laughs
Miraculous medicine of future and past
It all comes back around

Pendulum's sway of the rocking horse
There's never just one linear course
There're times to flow and times to force
As the leaves turn from green to unseen
It all comes back around

Entrusting in the paths you chose
What's 'round the bend, no one knows
Whether life is poetry or prose
Hair comes and goes but always grows
It all comes back around

Sycamores spiralling to the ground
It all comes back around

ROAMING WITH YOU

Music by **Sylvia Stella**
Words by **Sylvia Stella** *&* **Seki Lynch**

She tried to leave by the back door of the cellar
My watch stopped three times before I let her
I saw her last night kissing her new fella
Now she's the skeleton under my umbrella

> I know there's a gypsy in you
> When we were young she showed me her truths
> I've been alone all about
> But now I'm calling her out
> Because I want to go a-roaming with you

She went to Michigan to try and find the one
She told him her secrets lived under his thumb
When she came back she chewed a different brand of gum
And by the Autumn she'd married his son

> I know there's a gypsy in you
> When we were young she showed me her truths
> I've been alone all about
> But now I'm calling her out
> Because I want to go a-roaming with you

I'm quitting cigarettes for a day
You wouldn't know me now—my habits have changed
So I walk barefoot by the laundry chute
Because your laces wouldn't fit in my travelling boots

I know there's a gypsy in you
When we were young she showed me truths
I've been alone all about
But now I'm calling her out
Because I want to go a-roaming with you

I STILL WANNA BE YOURS

With thanks to John Cooper Clarke

You're the firefly to my glass jar
The engine to my fast car
Like a world-class golfer
You're always above par
You're the genie in my lamp
You're the box to my tramp
If I'm caught short in the woods
I think of you and I glamp
When I'm feeling well dim
You keep my thoughts bright
When I wake with a fright
You're more comfort than a furry night light
You're the kite of my loins
You make me want to fly low
With you, there's no escape
Cupid int an archer, she's got a crossbow

I still wanna be yours

If I won a million quid, you'd be the first one I'd call
I'm never in the gnome, you make me feel twelve feet tall
I left you once cos I thought I was no good
I was thicker in me 'ed than a 2 x 4 of wood

Cos I cunt deny it then and I can't deny it now
So I'll make you a mountain out of this molehill, somehow
I hope I'll always be able to make you blush
And that when I get me mitts on you, you still feel a rush

Here's a soppy love poem for you, my little cauliflower
Guess where I'm heading when I leave work in an hour?

I still wanna be yours

No doctor can nurse the knocking of me heart
It meks a proper racket any time we're apart
They can't tell what it is, but I know the prognosis
'Cos for you I'll bend over backwards
        like av gotta rare form of scoliosis
I'll eat up your bogies and I'll drink up your tears
Whatever it takes to keep you near to here
I'm a Lone Ranger—a longing desperado
With just one shot left, so here goes
Am going against the universe, breaking Newton's famous law
You're the apple of my sky

I still wanna be yours

TEETH

I want someone who has lived through their teeth
Give me years of red wine, late nights, laughter
Nut-brown crema, coffee-invaded crags
Yellow staining, turmeric on light palms
The wilt of magnolia in Autumn—
Evidence of tobacco smoke inhaled
From baby-bright milk squares to gold-capped decay
Bottles opened in the park; cracked crab shells
Tell me of trouble with rich fatty meat
Steak stuck between maxillary molars.
That they left their mark in many lovers
I'm not jealous, allow them adventure
Give me the bloodstained teeth of a huntress
The teeth of a revolutionary

FLOWERS

Darling,

After thinking about it too much
And talking about it too long
I finally went to the supermarket
And bought you flowers

They weren't the cheapest
Because the cheap ones looked shitty
Which is why I didn't want to buy flowers
From the supermarket

I picked the roses because I think,
Though cliché, they're the best flowers
To give a lover
I picked the ones which look like sunflowers
Because I remembered you like sunflowers

On my way home I saw a girl in tears.
She looked like she'd just discovered heartbreak
And I couldn't help but give her the flowers
For hope
Knowing if I told you this
You'd believe me
And you'd be happy I was thinking of you
Even as I was thinking of someone else

UNSAID

I once was your guardian
I, happy Atlas, you, my world
I held you proudly with gentle hands
Receiving wise gifts from a girl

You once were my defender
A fierce knight dressed in yourself
Knowing only how to care
And in these fair lands, we dwelt

Many years passed in peacetime
Many years passed in war
But through it, we rowed together
Our hands blistered by the oars

The sands of time outlived the hourglass
The sands of time buried us both
'Til our bodies' presents became past
And our lives returned to Earth

But still then, there was no rupture
No crack marred our waxen shell
Through heaven and earth, we journeyed
Served our obligatory slice in hell

I once had an idea
About freedom from all things
I tried to escape myself first

Drinking myself into dreams

And when I found I was trapped in me
I considered freedom from you
The self I was you knew too well
Without you, I could be new

And this thought grew and grew
An atom of doubt became true

The morning came when I told you
I made you avocado and eggs on bread
I watched you leave with your suitcase
Holding so many words unsaid

I once had your love inside me
Now I'm full of booze and smoke
Anything I can to blind me
To stop me seeing what I broke

LEFT ME HERE

Verse 1

I keep a needle and thread
In my heart box
To darn your socks
My love

I keep asking myself
Will the reel ever run out?

I spend my days cleaning up
Your breadcrumbs
Why do you leave such a mess?
Pup

I just want to come home
But you never cut me a key

Bridge
Ooo you've got me wrapped around your pinkie
You're so, cool
So damn cool
x2

Chorus
It's what you did my love
It's what you did,
Not what you said...
It's what you did
My love
Not what you said

You left me here for dead
Left me here for dead
My love,
Left me here for...

Verse 2

In the water I swam
Against the little hooks of your love
Dove

But they tired me out
Just like you knew they would

I spend my nights going through
What I do
Why can't you ever stay around?
Boo

I'm left hanging on the line
Caught in your winds every time

Bridge
Ooo you've got me wrapped around your pinkie
You're so, cool
So damn cool
x2

Chorus

It's what you did my love
It's what you did,
Not, what you said
It's what you did
My love
Not what you said
It's what you did
What you did
My love
You left me here for dead

Outro
Do you remember what you said?
But you left me here for dead...
My love
Left me here for...

HOME

The generous sun's rays are not infinite
But look how it spends them on us daily

The river faithfully pours itself out
That it might once again be filled up

The song gives itself to the listener
Tucked inside the listener keeps it safe

When we started to build this place between us
It was as instinctive as birds first nesting
Anything might become part of this place

Bring us our tools
Cry work-eager hands

The universe sends itself out into the unknown
It's gathering is an act of creation

Into one another we patiently dig
Just a trowelful is enough to grow a garden
Imagine what might bloom in a lifetime

We were two snowflakes in the blizzard
Until we melted back into the sea

Do you remember anything
Before we got home?

STRINGS

From silence to a rumble
Big bang cosmic reverb from your stare
The same frequency the Quaker takes
From Earth in prayer
This was how our symphony began
With the fingers of the universe
Playing the strings of your hair

Your eyes are lifting snare cracks
Striking with the ferocity of bomb blasts
Your eyes are shimmering cymbal rings
Tolling an end to my past
They are the bass drum
Speaking every primal language without tongue
The same language of cries and laughs

Your digits trace my fingers and palms
Each of your ridges intersects my lines playing tunes
You play the records of my life
A gramophone needle to my grooves
Every one of my personal notes
You create a unique signature
For every single mood
To my rhythm and my blues

Your smile is an oboe with soft vibrato
An early summer walk down boulevards
Guiding the adventurous spirit:
As the world turns underfoot–nothing's far

The brilliance of your happiness in bloom
Fills my mind's sky with galaxies
Snowflakes on tar

The heart is made of infinite instruments
Delicate, durable, sensitive as a still lake
To an icicle's drop or a surfacing fish
One fine pluck is all it takes
Its chambers are full of rhyme
And its beating knows no reason
Only that another beats
Therefore it must beat in time

The Earth vibrates
And everything comes around
To rest in the silence created
After the quake

SNARE

I have been the deer
In the woods
In the evening

Moonlight lit my bleeding leg ensnared

And I called to anything to put me out
But no hunter came
No god answered

And I'm glad

KIN

You began in fire
A white crack in grey sky
Beetle-bore cone dried in flames
You fell, to the burnt firs beneath
Still warm, you lay nestled in their heat
Back as a germ
As a seedling
You pushed and kicked
Embryonic
Waking in the darkened womb of the earth
The burnt womb brought your birth

The birds swooped still and chirped
And beaked earthworms while you watched.
Rivers ran against salmon streams
Retracing aeons, as your ancestors looked on.
The sun, ever elder, spilt blood into firmament
And you drew in all that would sustain
Until only you remained

Later you took nourishment from fog
The great mystic of the woods
Keeping your evergreens cloaked
As moonlight lit clouds 'round your branches.
And in the quiet the owl's flight
As the crickets mocked the morning
You knew the world had been waiting for you
Before the dawn bird, before the bat flew

Later still, wind brought knowledge to your leaves
Everything from screams to whispers
Taught you things you'd never know:
The secrets of sleep. Of canopy, cave and seabed
And you, Sequoyah, made the language of Wisdom
Wrote it in rings, in circles, as you aged
Breeze-blown breaths first and last
Visions in the present and dreams of the past

Years later, cool night rested over the wood
Cooled your bole; cooled water in your xylem
But it was dry and fire came again.
Scorched your bark
Scorched where the carpenter ant and kin
Carved their names deep into you

Still, you grew
Still, you grew

I call you redwood
I call you redwood
I call you freedom
I call you love

SANTIAGO

On the fringes of diluting memory
I scrawl language indecipherable

(Palimpsest of unimaginable depths
In the unconscious cities of the undreaming)

Through an underwater maze
We swim
With the tyrants and soothsayers chasing us

Hell-bent on erasing us

We emerge beneath tracks
A train's passing
We wait

The train's passed
I climb onto the platform

Behind me, you try to climb out
You're exhausted
You're my exhausted heartbeat
And for the first time
I see you might not make it
You take my hand and I pull you up

I've got an idea
Or you had it first
Or also

Courage: This is madness
Courage: This is insane
Courage: This is impossible

Please Santiago
Please Santiago please

Please keep going

When I find you, I'll become a mother whale
I'll keep you buoyed on my back until
Pigment by pigment you disintegrate
Go back to the seas knowing how I called
I can't guide you now but keep going
There's a search party out there for you
They know your name

We court couples of beautiful women together
Hypnotised by their hair
We dance—hymns in forgetful snow
And melt the night
Unleashing some inner menagerie
Only to herd our animals
Back into the ark of our chest
And leave; forever alone

Destined to ourselves
It is only your hand in mine
As we outpace time

I once knew you by another name
Another and another and another
I find you again
And my heart breaks a little more
As it grows yet another hyphae
Reaching out to the source of myself
In a billion more bodies
..And here you are again
Reaching at me through the eyes

THIS IS HOW I FIND YOU

The liver works incessantly breaking
The bonds open, breaking open the bonds
The yeast breaks open sugar crystals searching
Had you forgotten my love? We're still searching
The liver works, hoping and hardening
Hardening and hoping, looking for you
A fatty organ dressed in mourning garb
In burnt incense and moonscape livery
Bilirubin foam bats internal shores
Corrupts integrity of cell walls
I'm polishing them trying to find you

I've seen the others searching in their way
Some farther, some nearer to their own shades
But this is how I find you

When the faithful grass comes bounding underfoot
I pet his shaggy coat and praise his green
I watch the moon rolling drolly on the hills
of time, never tiring of her game
I see placid clouds, albino sea cows
Grazing and gently panning through blue
Can you ever hear our voices through the rain?
On cosmos blown breath of winter stars
Our Earth, cocooned in ozone grape-skin thin
I draw pale blinds over absinthe-steeped eyes
Searching for shades of inner peace-spun light

These hues from cave wall pigments I translate
To canvas stretched over sanded frame
Neurotransmission voiced through timid brush
Solvent evaporates... beetle-shelled paints
Mind flaring–meteor scraping, lightless
Striving, circling globules into themselves
Spiralling
I draw closer

When I find you, I'll become a mother whale
I'll keep you buoyed on my back until
Pigment by pigment you disintegrate
Go back to the seas knowing how I called
I can't guide you now but keep going
There's a search party out there
They know your name

I've been meditating
In every way I've been meditating
This is how I find you

In how my knuckles trace across the trees
Ancestral bark of wrinkled fisher hands
In how my thigh expands, a tugging knot
Against the silken tread of time, running
Meditating

Beyond the reach of where my legs can carry
Light-spun ball of knotted muscular strength
This is how I find you
In how my tongue buds bloom in the lung breeze
Searching for you in every atom charge
In every scoop of air I'm blessed to breathe
Searching
Meditating
I've been meditating

I called upon the Sufis in their robes
Who painted their existence in footstrokes
In dark of my dimensions learnt your name
Echoing song tracing the planets' sway
I called on the silk kimonoed Ronin
Esters evaporating, spirits rising
From textured fabric, life-canvas stretched out,
Their smiling stomachs painted oily rose
Sickle sunset turned roses to gold

I asked everyone

The birds call well before the slip of dawn
In tone-shy light, in bashful monochrome
Repeating unselfconsciously they go
Repeating themselves frantically they call
Searching for you
We're all searching for you

The fox is vigilant, quick-eyed and slick
Red-tailed in his evening surveillance
Red-tails green bushes on his evening rounds
Searching for you

With capillaries, the small bones of the ear
The stirrups with their sonar poise
The olfactory bulbs shark-hungry
With these the party make their inquisitions
Hounding and sniffing; any rag of you
Truffle pigs of the party snuffling for you
Unconscious and uncounting of their trot
Their only knowing longing, untiring,
Unaware of how much farther or falter
Bodies know no pains, only thirst and longing
I go about knowing peace in no place
I'm turning myself inside out for you
Where are you hiding?

The roots of trees dig in the earth for you
Sifting through soil as sea stars comb through sand
I've been gathering
Meditating

The planets turn maddeningly, incessant,
Restlessly straining against practised physics
Their language unravelling and absorbed
By dark matter into black hole silence
The universe turning itself inside out
Language unspooling, neural chemicals

Panned with prayer for any clue of you
This is how I find you

You

Mirrored soul carp of indeterminate growth
Who swims obsidian space, ever-expanding
Refracting light from polished prism scales

SLAVE

Where once was clad the weight of iron chains
I'm a slave to the night
Slave to the sex
Slave till the grave

Where once whip-lashing marked rebellious ways
I salve scar tissue
With medicines which make thoughts fade

You'll still find me hanging:
Too cool for cool
Just another fool caricature
In a city too full of lights to shine

I'm getting on it at 11am
I'm staying on it at 11am
I'm going to work to start again
I'm the snatches of sleep in afternoon
I'm all of my insomniac dreams
I'm barely holding at the seams

PHANTOMS

As you followed the line of my finger
I realised I'd been given the gift
Of foresight to fill the void of all
That would no longer come to pass

The pheasant flapping past the windscreen
Cracking brittle air with long wing beats
Its form obscured by winter's grit
Unwiped, because busy as ever
I'd not added de-icer. The water froze

Now I see everything I'd have pointed to
Know all I'd have shown you
So acutely, with such at-once clarity
Some things can only be felt

Ripened berries hanging sun-swelled and stalk-fat,
Unpicked by the same right hand
Which kept my left company on so many journeys

The sights of future us—(dear friends) accompany me in clubs
Chaperone my taste changed meals alone
Babysit my balled-up nights
Serve me coffee and croissants come light

My companions leave me
Forever wringing myself out
For the company of our past

The melodies of memories
Stave off the clefts of time unspent

I hear the emotion in your voice
As you threaten the future doorman
For his conduct while kicking me out
Unjustly and before I've had a swig

How I laugh at your waddle
As we run for the last night bus
In the city which raised us
The city which watched us grow

If I'm haunted by anything
It's by the magic of our laughter
The flint of words spark incantations
Which invoke the spirit's roar

It's because of all this that I must let you go
Because I want more than
The ghost of a smell
The image of a presence
The cooling of after-touch.
Yet here I am still
Dancing to our beat
Solo

THE ICEBERG PRINCIPLE

The fans turn slowly in the restaurant as we drink. On our way to Pamplona to see the bulls run. Brett. Glass to lips sits with her napkin in her lap. The waiter comes. She laughs at his small talk. Happy to forget. We drink our drinks swiftly and order more when the bread comes. Tonight is just another night in our life of circles.

Brett asks for a pen while Mike smokes. She draws circles on the placemat. Then lights up a cigarette herself and starts on her new drink. The fans make shadows on the tablecloth as the sun leaves. As the night comes. More drinks arrive and Mike starts asking the same questions. Brett wants to run away. Her face tight. She had almost forgotten. She stands. Squeezes between chairs. Sits in his lap.

She lives in his lap. Sitting there her eyes move in circles over his face. Searching for something. A look he once had, forgotten. A look she replaces with champagne and drinks. It's cold now and her mascara is running. I call the waiter. He comes.

Something fast happens. Then the drink comes. I feel like the world is bent. I'm tired of running laps. Brett's strap falls from her shoulder. My mind is running after the drink in my head. Or the drink is after my mind. Either way, I can feel circles. She asks if I want another drink. I shrug and focus on Mike. I try to remember and forget. But I can't forget.

I think of fresh air and ask them to walk but only she comes. The air fills my head with the drink. I sway and fall, pulling her into my lap. I tell her a stupid truth. "We have come full circle." She laughs then gets up and runs.

I watch the past follow her as she runs. I stand and wonder if, like me, Mike would not forget. We are two overlapping circles. And here she comes skulking back like a cat, ready to curl up in my lap. We go back and she orders more drinks.

We live inside circles and things come back to run at us. Not allowing us to forget. Lapping against our minds like a sea of drink.

WINE AND JUG

Soul,

Remember.

Remember the time before mirages and visions and believing you can see things more than you can see.

Remember the time before self-hatred and self-deception. Before you had anything to hide. Before the self you saw was something you couldn't be.

Remember the other world where we were never separate. When we followed one another as the wine follows the jug.

We were once wine and jug. We journeyed together each as one. Remember our adventures as one.

And if we were unloaded we both cast one shadow. An image brought alive by the sun.

An image which graced our feet until we were stowed away again. Until we followed an unknown path once again.

We were drunk together for hours. Happily alone amongst the other urns, under the cool of a canvas sky.

Until one night we arrived, as we all do, at our place of parting. Taken to a rooftop where the tiles were cold and blue and the stone kept the heat of day long into night.

You were decanted and drunk by soldiers. To be emptied into pots or people or dust. I was left empty until broken, by a drunken fool who stumbled into the table at sunrise.

It will not be for a thousand lifetimes and we'll see many more in between.

But one day I will be wine and you will be jug. Opposite and same. You'll carry me inside your cool shell. We'll be together again.

I will be wine and you will be jug and we'll be drunk together again.

Until then, I'll wait here on this rooftop, buried two thousand years underground.

THE FEAST

When I dream I dream of you. All of you
I dream of a great table. A banquet in the forest
I dream of Xenia and of every guest playing host
A billion hands cooking favoured dishes
Laced with laughter, pricked and peppered with spices
Salted with tears, stocks thickened with blood
And of course, you're there too, as I knew you would be

Eyes dizzy with love

The great banquet table
Laid with porcelain jugs fashioned as fish
Mosaic plates of familiar patterns
Cutlery which fits as if smithed for bearer's hands
Napkins of fine linen—at a touch—we remember other
lives

Usually so careful of words
I dream of you and they pour from me
On hearing these, your own thoughts spill out
The banquet is our secret and our telling of it
Reunited, the dogs in our chests curl upon themselves
To settle flop-eared into their corners of the heart

Already the wine is flowing
I slip out unnoticed among the bustling
The dancing and the singing
In the forest-garden, I slow by the waterfall
Which is breathing in the silence of the moonlight

Far from the gathering; only the tender water's hushing
As it tries to restrain the excitement of meeting with itself
In the water's mirrored tryst—the sohbet of the party

Back at the feast
A furnace of mingling and flirting and charms exchanged
Essential metal is being formed
Each guest, alchemist and mineral
Polished mirror and reflected gold

As we eat we begin to forget
We forget our age and begin to lose our accents
When asked, we can't recall our favourite song
We forget our names and the names of our beloveds
We forget our self-consciousness and our scars
Empty and full, our laughter flows
We forget ourselves and clamber onto the table
The wine too flows and we guests begin to embrace
We merge as fire meets fire
In reuniting, we realise we were never apart
A foot tips a candle; the tablecloth catches
We are the threads and the flames
Crackling into ever-being
A drunken inferno

SOHO MISSES YOU

The thought of you got me up again today.
Light shafts on fall leaves in your streets.

As I brushed my teeth, street sweepers in luminous jackets
Scrubbed gutter foam over tarmac as traffic creeped.

As I did my tie, sweet Thames played the blues through you.
All your winding clefts, all your bars I knew.

The thought of you got me up again today
Just thinking about the person I could be
In the heart of the city.
The person I could become in your streets

Great city, you have my heart
Take me
Home

'OUMUAMUA

'Oumuamua or 1I/2017 U1 is the first confirmed interstellar object to visit our Solar System. This rocky, cigar-shaped object, with a somewhat reddish hue, was named 'Oumuamua by its discoverers. The word loosely translates to 'scout' from Hawaiian (reaching out, in advance of).

Rotating in a manner we Earthlings
Describe as irregular
An object from outer space
Visits close enough to our tiny home
For us to burst into activity across the planet
And take terrible pictures
With our high-resolution telescopic cameras.
On the asteroid-like lump
Which doesn't behave like an asteroid at all
Is an information-capture system
Similar to our video cameras and voice recorders, But
which receives and transmits dark matter
Pure consciousness

The trajectory of the object is no chance happening.
A calculated course positions 'Oumuamua
Far enough away to react to pulsar attack
But close enough to investigate
The densely concentrated consciousness cloud emitted
By our blue-green blob.
The object absorbs
The inner juju of mind-spirit
And reverberates at these frequencies
Broadcasting into the neverness of space.
All is received at once
Just as three objects
Dropped one after another

Reach the ground
At the same time
Past, present, future, scrambled egg.
'Oumuamua takes in the Dream Time
The world began with a song
The ancestors sang each rock, tree, river
Into existence
Until song, nothing existed
When the song stops
All disappears

'Oumuamua takes in the 5 suns of the Aztecs
Four preceding races, then our own
The race of giants, killed by jaguars
The race of people killed by hurricane
The race of people killed by god-fire
The race of people submerged in 52 years of god-blood tears
They survived drowning by becoming fish.
We the final race are only sustained by human sacrifice
This we take to with religious zeal

In Mali, man was made of stone, iron, water, fire, air
In his pride man was made blind
Blindness's pride led to sleep
Sleep to worry, worry to death
Eventually, the eternal one came down
And defeated death.

At once these stories are taken in
with a Tanzanian creationist myth

Shida Matunba has two wives
His favourite dies
She is buried in the house
Shida waters her grave in grief

Certain his wife will rise again
And forbids the second wife from going near.
A plant begins to grow
One day Shida leaves the house
The second wife sneaks in to see the grave
In jealousy, she hacks the plant with a hoe
Blood gushes from the grave filling the house.

"The world is just a simple circle."

'Oumuamua takes all in.
At any one time
A billion faces are sucked into cameras at the speed of Zoom...
A continuous consciousness current ad infinitum
Beneath our feet, mycelium divert nutrients
Along single-celled logistical superhighways

At our fingertips, we have connected all consciousness
Double mycelium envelopes our planet
Twice sealed in an interconnected intelligence
One organic. The other man-made
THE INTERNET!
How old were you when you saw the woman
Being fucked to death by a horse?
This is the greatest technological advancement
Since the atomic bomb
What do you reckon our insides look like?

"Peace Mercutio peace
Thou speaks of nothing."

On your birthday
I ran you a bath and washed your hair
And told you to close your eyes
That all you had to do now
Was just listen to the sound of my voice

And the circling of suds on the backs of your ears
All you had to do was listen
And focus on the sensation
Of my three-day-clipped fingers nails
Massaging your scalp
If you did that
And just focussed on my voice
I'd make it all go away.

When the baby first kicks
The song in the child's heart
Depends on which foot the mother is on
And where she is standing
My mother was on her left foot
Stood on the mosaic tile
Of a bird or paradise
Under the pillar which Rumi circled
Laughing for having known Shams
And grieving that he'd gone

On a gas-guzzling yacht in the Mediterranean
A sommelier studiously opens a bottle with a curt hiss
50% Pinot Noir 50% Chardonnay grape

Aged on the lees for 18 months the liquid has a straw hue
The aging has lent the wine warm toasted brioche notes
Buttered croissant.
The iced champagne
Mixed with the sea air
And the persistent shaved truffle
From a decadent spread
Showered in Vitamin D
Has the effect of well-placed thumbs
On the trapezium muscles.
Life is good.

"In this civilisation a man who cannot support his wife and
his child is not a man."

'Oumuamua takes in thought

I'm running
I still think about it when I'm running
Your hand around my throat
Was I ten yet?
I've trained my whole life
To be able to stand up to you
I'm still running
I run against the ghost of the past
With the force of a speeding comet
Willing myself to create a different future
Comet-like, I obey orbit
The future is a merry-go-round

"The more I try to erase you
The more, the more
The more that you appear."

Turn left, then turn left
You have missed your exit please make a U-turn

Korean Budae Jjigae bubbling
On the screen Anthony Bourdain
Spills soy sauce on a computer mouse.
Some of our species kill themselves
Because they cannot bear to be here
Any longer.
Kalief Browder
Hanged himself at 22
Ravaged by a soulless
System

In a past life
I'd have been a samurai
Alive at the end of battle.
Captive.
Soaked in shame.
Allow me my wakizashi
That I might address my disgrace.

"I really don't care, do you?"
Melania Trump's coat blows in the wind.

Dawww look at him
Awww bless
Daww, he can't breathe again
Dawww look at him trying
Oooop, oooop.
Dawwww, he couldn't do it could he.

"Black bodies swinging in the Southern breeze
Strange fruit hanging from the poplar trees."

You may not see the moon
But she's there

There's always been a giant black hole
In the centre of our galaxy
One day, the earth will enter it
And we have no idea what will happen then
We might have to live it all again

Creation is an act of rebellion against death
Consumption is a form of death
I'm worried I can't do it
Accomplish composing the song in my heart
But Miss Simone says, "No fear. Freedom means no fear."
And to the gods that do and don't exist I want our freedom
I'm going to sing all of our ancestors into existence

'Oumuamua takes in the quiet strings of the heart

"The world is just a simple circle, circle."
"Your suffering does not isolate you. Your suffering is
your bridge."
"We must corner ourselves to make a new assumption."

I still believe in the life force
That drives so many in the face of adversity

'Oumuamua sees with at once clarity
The ebb and flow of nature
Birth and death are spinning plates
Snail-porcelain crushed accidentally underfoot
At once streamed into 'Oumuamua
The countless dying
On David Attenborough programmes
On smartphones
On the rising coastal planes
In the Momento Mori
We fetishize what we fear
This is exactly what it means to be alive
Death is coming
Till then, is what we have good enough?

I still believe
In the animal joy
Of thinking about you in a David Hockney swimming pool
Like a shining golden otter
I can't wait to run you a bath on your birthday

You can just listen to the birds chirp
At 5:06 in the morning
Whether this is a gift
Or rubs you up the wrong way
Is up to you
Sufis still exist

There are still some here who believe
In spite of fear
We can sing our way through life
They can't quiet
All our voices

'Oumuamua listens

'Oumuamua hears

'Oumuamua hopes

MUSIC BOX

From the moon, the earth
Through clouds
A car on tarmac
Naughty combustion vehicles
We can't help ourselves—cars and fuel make money!
Peel the Mitsubishi open like a sardine tin
There is a human operating the combustion vehicle
With the aid of spectacles
Last year he found a lump between his testicles
But now everything's fine
The car tank is nearly full
The man is full
Next to him is a female specimen
She had to poke a new hole in her belt
With a knife, which she enlarged with a chopstick
YES!!!! SUCCESS!
She'll be failing again by autumn
The two have had a row but his left hand
Has found hers halfway home
Simply Red is playing—they begin to sing:
"And Iiiiiii want to fall from the stars "
In the rear seats are their offspring
Two little boys
The music is breathing into their dreams
The colours their consciousness perceive in dream
Are electrical signals jumping between synapses?
Might these colours affect the proteins of the heart?
How many beats in a lifetime?
At any one time how many beat in chorus?

At this very moment
How many of your hearts are beating
In perfect synchronicity?
At this very moment
My heart is in time with a gazelle's
I have never had the pleasure of meeting.
The tail of the humpback beats the ocean
Brothers and sisters of sea-scape
The wing of the hummingbird beats the atomic
  composition of our atmosphere
Tiny elders of the air
We should teach Heathcote William's Whale Nation to
  five-year-olds
Humans spend their lives making money
Prince is dead
The music lives on on wax vinyl
Which you have no idea how to make
You can watch a video of a vinyl
Being pressed on YouTube
But you won't—I wouldn't
The time of your life is expanding and contracting
Music is vibration
Everything vibrates
Everything you love is singing
The whole universe is singing
"I've been down so god damn long
That it looks like up to me."

Once upon a time
A little boy fell asleep
In the cinema
The silver screen
Mingled with his dreams
The Dalai Lama is still a refugee

There are fungi, which infect ants
And inspire in them an irresistible urge
To climb as high as possible.
Once the fungus has driven a host ant
To an optimum location
At the height of the jungle canopy
Ant secures purchase by locking
Its mandibles into the vein of the leaf.
Here the fungus mummifies the ant
And in fruiting
Bursts through its exo-skull
From this great height, the spores of the fungus
Can spread much further
In search of other hosts.
But the fungi are humane
They do not mock the ants by making them dance
Before turning them into decaying taxidermy

Yesterday Violet passed away. Soho girl. 92.
When I met her, at 87, she'd just taken up smoking.
Menthol Dunhill Super Kings
"I've never smoked in all my life," she'd say as she took a
drag, pissed, sipping a gin and tonic.
Or, "I had the best years of my life in the war. Oooo yeah.
People always coming and going here and there.
Really exciting."
We asked her about the soldiers. She became shy and
fobbed us off like we were being
naughty.

We loved her.
Until we bought her that fucking bell!

I told you I loved you in Liverpool
On New Year's Eve
MDMA helped me get past myself
I'd been so scared to tell you
You became every character in my heart
Now everything is on fire
And I want every bridge to burn
Except the one that leads back to you
The smoke of our love is still in the air
And both the sky and I are blue
I'll hold my breath for a thousand years
For a chance to be your mermaid
I can barely speak
We can't be together
But if the world is good
When this all ends, I'd love to cook you dinner

If anything happens to me
Tell her she was it.

Western life goals
Put your penis in as many witches as possible
If their hearts break, so what?
We're all going to die anyway
If one puts a spell on you
Place a small trinket of earth ore on her finger
And make her believe you've lost your eyes
To a small winged baby with a crossbow
Accumulate as much wealth
Through as many avenues as possible

Belittle them into submission
If Mother Earth gets in your way
Fuck the cunt
Let her bleed

You have to be mad to survive here
Survival of the sickest
The rappers learnt it from the establishments
Survival of the sickest
Bring forth all the illegal medicines
To help me forget how I got here
I'm so sick
If I hadn't been deprogrammed of the courage
I'd have marched to parliament
Wearing a dove as a kerchief
Singing some old peace myth
Because the old bridges still exist, for now
If they burn the rest
If they burn all the bridges
Meet me underground with Rumi
"Seeds must hide in the ground
To become whatever is in them."
Cool and damp down there
As the world burns
How are we ever going to find our way back?
The story of a life
That isn't mine
Began as a dream I once had
When I woke
—I can't wake—
But when I woke
There was a door

To wake
All I had to do was
Was...
I've forgotten

"Don't worry, about a thing,
Because every little thing
Gonna be alright."

I don't know how to tell people
About this dream
I'm full of unreal dreams
I keep hoping I will wake up
Yawning
In the back of my parents' car
With Simply Red playing
In every deep breath of air
We breathe in ten fungal spores
Fungal spores have entered and exited
The lungs of every animal that has ever taken a breath of
    earth air
Spores have journeyed to the ocean depths
In the respiratory systems of Cuvier's beaked whale
Spores have been carried across continents on the winds

There was a time when the winds did not exist
There will be a time when the winds no longer exist
Between then and then
How many beats?
How many choruses?
Until then
As bad as it may get

We can't help ourselves
Here we are
Singing

THE CLOCKS STOP

With all these clocks
It's hard to keep time with the universe

I search faces
Trying to recall when we met

Time was an inside joke we made up
So we could keep playing
Whilst the rest of the world slept

We have always been in this place
And will remain here

Well after the last tick

EQUANIMITY

Written for the Ancient Infinity Orchestra's song Equanimity on their album River of Light.

Peace at dawn
Peace on the winds
Peace enters the body through root branches as we sing

Peace in the sunlight
Peace in the breeze
Peace flowing freely through the currents of the seas
Peace

There are bombs forever falling
Hearts eternally breaking
Bodies born in unique forms
The mind's riverways misshapen
Through blades of grass on tyrant's lawns
Fungus controlled ant and stillborn
Grief-stricken and dementia-adorned
Soul-torn fabric of kin who mourn
Peace

Capsized rafts and mortgage foreclosures
Alluvial soils when flood banks spill over
Skeletal forms of the white cliffs of Dover
The last blast of a star as it turns supernova
Peace

Longing for sleep when the mind's racing
Plastic-thick water in the river's basin
Scarring of tissue as the liver's decaying

Cancer-rich blood of the leukaemia patient
Every flag of every nation
Peace

Conquest after conquest
Oedipus complex
Conflicting ideologies
Emotional distress
Militias during civil unrest
Relentless images of death
Mediums comforting the bereft

In all this, your very existence is progress
Peace

Take it from the sun
Take it from the rain
Take it from the breath
It's woven in the pain
Peace

Take it from the sun
Take it from the rain
Take it from the breath
It's woven in the pain
Peace

Take it from the sun
Take it from the rain
Take it from the breath
It's woven in the pain
Peace

ALSO AVAILABLE FROM SALAMANDER STREET

All Salamander Street books can be bought in bulk at a discount for performance or study. Contact info@salamanderstreet.com to enquire about performance licenses.

CELINE'S SALON VOLUME 1
ISBN: 9781838403638

An anthology of work by 29 writers, songwriters and artists who have performed at Soho's literary cabaret Celine's Salon.

CELINE'S SALON VOLUME 2
ISBN: 9781739103026

Poetry, short-stories and song lyrics from 29 contributors to Celine's Salon.

JUAN BY JUAN by Juan Ramirez, Jr.
ISBN: 9781914228971

A collection that explores life, identity and love by Puerto Rican and Guatemalteco, Bronx born and raised, Juan Ramirez, Jr.

HOPE IS A SILHOUETTE by Lana McDonagh
ISBN: 9781739103019

A body of intimate and introspective poetry with accompanying illustrations, both written and painted by Lana McDonagh.

RAFFERY'S RULES by Frank Rafferty
ISBN: 9781738429363

Glaswegian-born, Derry-based performance poet Frank Rafferty shares his comic musings coupled with political calls to action in this debut poetry collection.

i am ill with hope by Gommie
ISBN: 9781914228575

Gommie's journey through poems and illustrations, offering bitesize snapshots of hope.